Where Is the Mississippi River?

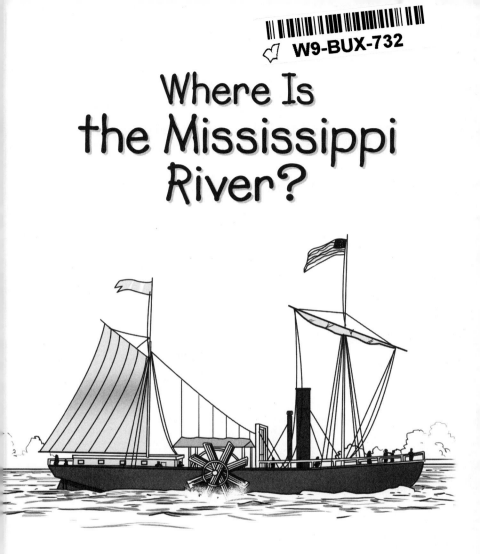

by Dina Anastasio

illustrated by Ted Hammond

Penguin Workshop
An Imprint of Penguin Random House

For Collin, Maggie, Christopher, and Nicholas,
who see the Mississippi River every day, and
for Jane O'Connor, my amazing editor—DA

To my mom—TH

PENGUIN WORKSHOP
Penguin Young Readers Group
An Imprint of Penguin Random House LLC

Library of Congress Cataloging-in-Publication Data is available.

ISBN 9780515158243 (paperback)   10 9 8 7 6 5 4 3 2 1
ISBN 9780515158267 (library binding)   10 9 8 7 6 5 4 3 2 1

Contents

Where Is the Mississippi River?

On July 4, 2002, a forty-seven-year-old man named Martin Strel took a swim in a small lake—Lake Itasca—in northern Minnesota. Lake Itasca is where the Mississippi River begins. It is the top of the river, which ends 2,350 miles farther south in the Gulf of Mexico.

Martin Strel had always loved being in the water. As a child in the Central European country of Slovenia, he had spent most of his time swimming in streams and lakes and rivers. When he wasn't swimming, he spent his time reading. He loved to read about rivers. He was fascinated by faraway rivers like the Danube in Europe, the Yangtze in China, the Amazon in South America, and the Mississippi River in the United States.

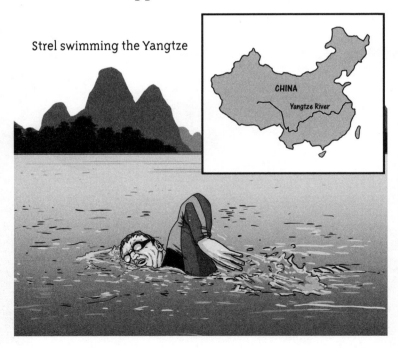

Strel swimming the Yangtze

CHINA

Yangtze River

One of his favorite books was called *The Adventures of Huckleberry Finn*, by Mark Twain. It was about a boy growing up beside the Mississippi River in Missouri. Huckleberry Finn takes a trip down the river on a raft. *Someday I will swim in that river*, Martin Strel thought.

Martin Strel never forgot his dream. Someday he would swim the entire length of the world's great rivers, from the top to the bottom. Martin kept training. In the year 2000, he swam the Danube River, through ten European countries. One thousand eight hundred sixty-six miles in fifty-eight days. No one had ever swum so far in such a short time.

After that, Martin was determined to swim the Mississippi. No one had ever done that before, either.

Martin learned all he could about the river. Like all rivers, the Mississippi twists and turns and shifts and changes as it flows south, so it is hard to pinpoint its exact length, but Martin knew he would be swimming about 2,350 miles. He was hoping to swim from five to twelve hours a day.

Martin began his swim at noon on July 4, 2002. People cheered him on from the banks of the river. He swam through or around in ten states—

Minnesota, Wisconsin, Iowa, Illinois, Missouri, Kentucky, Tennessee, Arkansas, Mississippi, and Louisiana. Martin didn't quite finish in as short a time as he had hoped. He swam for sixty-eight days instead of sixty-six.

Today, as Martin Strel swims the world's rivers, he works to help people understand the importance of clean water.

"My target is to see happy fish swimming in the water," he says.

Swimming Rivers

After the Mississippi, Martin Strel kept on swimming big rivers: the Paraná River in Argentina: 1,200 miles in twenty-four days; the Yangtze River in China: 2,487 miles in fifty-one days; the Vltava River in the Czech Republic: 226 miles in seven days; the Drava River in Central Europe: 280 miles in seven days; and the Amazon River in South America: 3,274 miles in sixty-six days, setting the world record for longest swimming journey.

CHAPTER 1
The Mighty Mississippi

The Mississippi River is not the longest river in the United States. (The Missouri River is longer.) But it is the most famous and it has played a large and exciting part in United States history. Many Americans think of the Mississippi as dividing the eastern and western halves of the country. They describe it as having three parts— the upper, middle, and lower.

The Upper Mississippi runs from Lake Itasca to Saint Louis, Missouri, where it meets up with the Missouri River.

Lake Itasca is 1,475 feet above sea level. That means water flowing from the lake will drop down 1,475 feet by the time it reaches the Gulf of Mexico. Think of a single drop of water moving from the top of the river to the bottom. That drop of water will take about ninety days to complete its journey. (Remember, it took Martin Strel only sixty-eight days.)

Lake Itasca is the narrowest part of the river. Leaving the lake, the river water meanders gently east for about sixty miles, where it passes through another Minnesota lake—Lake Winnibigoshish. (Try saying that three times fast!) At that point, it is about eleven miles wide, the widest part of the river. From there on, the water begins its long drop to the Gulf. Catfish, paddlefish, walleye, carp, bass, and pike swim there. Kayaks and canoes paddle through whirlpools, waterfalls, weeds, and rain along streams and lakes too shallow for the barges and steamboats that work the river farther south.

Walleye

In the busy Twin Cities of Saint Paul and Minneapolis, the river becomes deeper. Larger boats carry people and goods south, past small towns and acres of farmland.

The Missouri River drains into the Mississippi from the west, just north of Saint Louis, Missouri.

The Middle Mississippi runs from Saint Louis to Cairo, Illinois, past lush farmland and small towns. This stretch is not long—only 190 miles—and doesn't twist and turn.

In Cairo, the Ohio River drains in from the east and the Lower Mississippi begins. This part of the river runs from Cairo to the Gulf of Mexico. One thousand miles. It flows past Memphis, Tennessee; Natchez, Mississippi; and New Orleans, Louisiana.

South of New Orleans, the Mississippi continues for another one hundred miles. This is a vast area of shifting wetlands called the Mississippi River delta. The delta has been forming for about

Delta wetlands

seven thousand years as mud, sand, rocks, and dirt spill from the river. Thirteen thousand square miles of rich, fertile forests, marshes, swamps, islands, and open water.

Fresh water and
saltwater come together
here. Migrating birds
stop here. Endangered species
like Louisiana black bears and green sea turtles
struggle to survive here. Shrimp,
oysters, tuna, and other fish

live here. Cattails, spider lilies, and other plants thrive. Alligators slide in and out of the water. Many people live in this area as well.

Finally, after more than two thousand miles, the Mississippi River reaches the Gulf of Mexico and comes to an end.

CHAPTER 2
A River Is Born

Before there was the Mississippi River, there was ice. Twenty-one thousand years ago, huge, massive, pointy sheets of ice called *glaciers* covered most of what is now the northern United States. The glaciers were thousands of feet thick. The

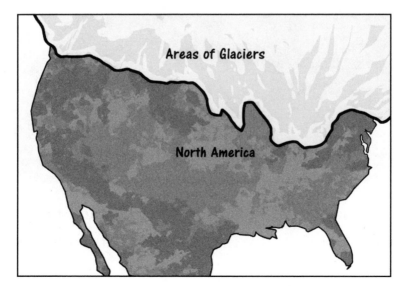

Areas of Glaciers

North America

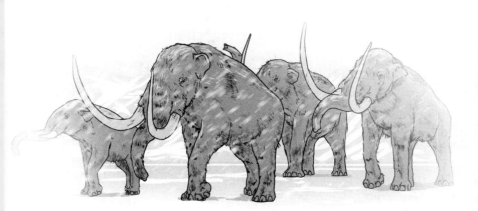

A herd of mastodons crossing a plain of ice

temperature was so cold that only giant animals able to hold in a lot of body heat could survive. Woolly mammoths, caribou, and mastodons roamed the edges of the glaciers. The world was in the middle of an ice age.

Paleo-Indians were the first known people to live along the Mississippi River. They survived by hunting the giant animals and dressing in warm furs and skins.

Then, the world began to warm again. Glaciers started to melt. Shards of ice and melting water began to move south, carving channels in the land.

As the giant glaciers melted, people came from far away to the newly created river. Most survived by hunting and fishing in the river. Later, the world grew warm enough to grow crops like beans and corn and pumpkins. The people in the area formed groups or tribes. Several tribes, including the Sioux, Choctaw, Natchez, Osage, and Ojibwa, took up farming.

Before long, villages were springing up along the upper, middle, and lower parts of the river.

Some members of the Ojibwa tribe settled in northern Minnesota where the Crow Wing River feeds into the Mississippi. They must have admired the river a great deal because they named it *Misi-ziibi*, which means "great river" or "gathering of water." From the Ojibwa comes the name *Mississippi*.

CHAPTER 3
Exploring the River

Because of the voyages of Christopher Columbus in the late 1400s, the people of Europe began to learn about a vast continent—North America. According to stories, it was a land of untold riches. Especially gold.

Kings and queens wanted to claim this rich land for their country. So they sent out explorers. Hernando de Soto was a Spanish soldier. He was not from a rich family, so the promise of gold interested him. In 1514, when he was about fourteen years old, he left on the first of many

Hernando de Soto

voyages to the New World. By 1539, de Soto was in command of a ship. He and his men arrived in what is now the state of Florida in search of gold. When they didn't find any, they continued farther west, fighting and capturing natives as they went.

On May 8, 1541, de Soto and his four hundred troops were making their way through the Arkansas wilderness when they spotted the Mississippi River. De Soto is said to be the first European to see it.

After the discovery, the men crossed the river in rafts and other flatboats. They waited until dark so they wouldn't be spotted by natives out in canoes who'd be carrying weapons. Once on the other side, they explored parts of what is now Louisiana, searching for gold and silver. Eventually they turned back toward the river, where Hernando de Soto died of a fever on May 21, 1542. He was buried in the river.

Father Jacques Marquette

About 130 years later, in 1673, two French explorers set out to learn where the Mississippi ended. By this time there were many colonies of European settlers in North America— both in what is now the eastern United States and also to the north in land that became Canada. Jacques Marquette was from France. He was a priest. Louis Joliet lived in Canada and worked as a fur trader. They wanted to know if the river flowed straight south to the Gulf of Mexico, or if it twisted and turned through the West and emptied

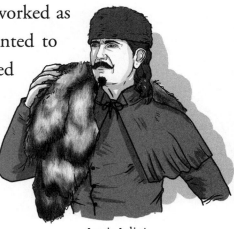

Louis Joliet

into the Gulf of California near the Pacific Ocean. Louis Joliet and Father Jacques Marquette decided to canoe down the river and find out. They had a small group of other explorers with them.

On the way, they stopped in Native American villages, bringing gifts and offering prayers. One friendly Illinois Indian tribe welcomed them with a ceremony during which they were given a *calumet* (peace pipe). Later, this same peace pipe saved their lives when they offered it to the chief of a tribe that was about to attack.

The Peace Pipe Ceremony

The passing of the calumet was a sacred Indian ceremony of friendship. To begin, the best morsels of food were presented to the guests. This meal was followed by speeches and the slow calumet dance. Then the chief of the tribe presented the long, feathered pipe.

The villagers they met were generous and kind. Food was offered. Indian guides helped them with directions.

As they headed south, they passed deer and cattle and swans. They used nets to catch sturgeon for dinner.

In present-day Arkansas, Marquette and Joliet stopped at a village where the Quapaw people lived. The Quapaw welcomed them warmly and showed them around their long, wide bark cabins where they slept on raised beds. In some cabins, they saw large baskets made of cane filled with corn.

From the native people, Marquette and Joliet came to learn where the Mississippi ended. The river emptied into the Gulf of Mexico. So now the explorers knew what they had come to find out. But they did not get to see the river's end for themselves. The Quapaw suggested they turn around and head back north. It was dangerous to go farther south, they said. Armed Spanish settlers were there. Marquette and Joliet would be attacked. With the help of a young Indian guide, they located a quicker route back to Canada.

A few years later, in 1682, René-Robert Cavelier, Sieur de La Salle made a journey down the Mississippi River.

La Salle was a fur trader from France who was obsessed with exploring new places. As a young man, he moved to Montreal,

René-Robert Cavelier,
Sieur de La Salle

in eastern Canada. Indians from the Mohawk tribe told him about the great river that flowed through the middle of the land to the south. They thought it turned to the west at some point and continued all the way to a sea that would take him to China.

La Salle decided to see for himself. Joliet and Marquette had paddled down the river only as far as Arkansas. La Salle was determined to keep going wherever the river took him. La Salle and his men made it all the way to the bottom of the river.

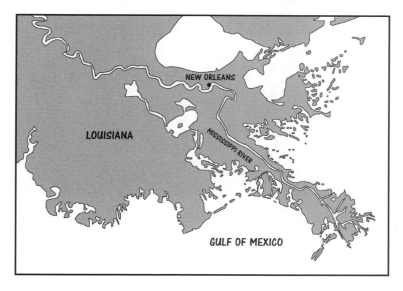

That settled it. The Mississippi River ended at the Gulf of Mexico, and France now claimed it. In honor of the French King Louis XIV, they named the land by the gulf Louisiana. A priest who was traveling with La Salle described the ceremony that followed: "On the ninth of April, with all possible solemnity, we performed the

ceremony of planting the cross and raising the
arms of France . . . the Sieur de la Salle, in the
name of his majesty, took possession of that river,
of all rivers that enter it, and of all the country
watered by [it]."

"All rivers that enter it"? "All of the country
watered by it"? In 1682, few people, including La
Salle, understood what that meant. Most of what
is now the United States had yet to be explored.

By 1762, this huge, vast part of the New World

had a name. It was called the Louisiana Territory. However, it no longer belonged to France. It belonged to Spain.

Settlers from British colonies along the Atlantic coastline were heading west. The Spanish didn't seem to mind people trading goods up and down their river, so this worked very well for about forty years.

Then, in 1800, everything changed again. France's new leader, Napoleon Bonaparte, wanted his land back. Spain agreed and signed it over.

Now, once again, France controlled the Mississippi River. Napoleon made it very clear that no one else but France could use the Port of New Orleans. In case anyone objected, Napoleon prepared his army to attack.

Napoleon Bonaparte

During this time, the coastal British colonies had become the United States of America. Thomas Jefferson was now president, and he was not going to stand for Napoleon's orders. He was ready to have American troops fight the French, but instead he came up with another plan. He offered to buy the entire Louisiana Territory from France.

Jefferson was sure that Napoleon would say no. But he was wrong. Napoleon agreed to sell. Diseases in the French West Indies were threatening his

French navy, and the French were not prepared to fight along the Gulf of Mexico. Also, England, as well as the United States, wanted the Louisiana Territory, and the British were willing to go to war to get it. Napoleon didn't want that.

France turned the vast 828,000–square mile Louisiana Territory over to the United States in the spring of 1803. The US government paid France $15 million, which at the time was about three cents an acre. It was the greatest bargain in the history of the New World.

Did France and the United States even have the right to make such a deal? Remember that Native American tribes had lived in this area for far, far longer than anyone else. Long before any European settlers arrived. But European countries, as well as the United States, never took this into account. They saw all this land in North America as theirs for the taking.

Fifteen States

In time, land in the Louisiana Territory became states or parts of states: all of Missouri (1821), Arkansas (1836), Iowa (1846), Kansas (1861), Nebraska (1867), and Oklahoma (1907); most of Colorado (1876), South Dakota (1889), Montana (1889), and Wyoming (1890); and parts of Louisiana (1812), Texas (1845), Minnesota (1858), North Dakota (1889), and New Mexico (1912).

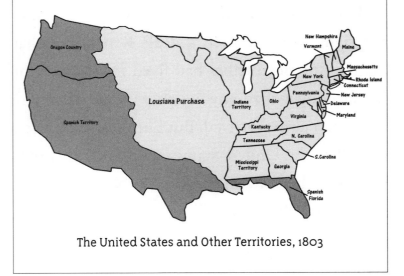

The United States and Other Territories, 1803

CHAPTER 4
Traveling the River

The Louisiana Purchase brought many changes to the United States. Settlers traveled west on land and water. Along rivers like the Ohio, boats filled with people from the Northeast made their way to the Mississippi. Travelers from Georgia, South Carolina, and other Southern states came by way of the Gulf of Mexico to reach the Mississippi. New immigrants arrived from Europe. Some crossed the river and continued even farther west into the newly bought land. Others built homes along the banks of the river. Small towns appeared and became bigger. In time, cities arose.

Travel along the river began to change, too. Swift currents had always made traveling downriver easier and faster than going up the river. Early settlers had used homemade rafts and other flat-bottomed boats. They floated furs, flour, pork, and other goods quickly downriver where they would be sold to Indians. But the return upriver, which went against the current, was often impossible for these vessels.

By 1800, keels, broadhorns, and other barges filled with coffee, sugar, cotton, logs, potatoes, lumber, furniture, and animals managed to get upriver, but it wasn't easy. Men  pushed long shoulder poles along the bottom of the river to keep the boats moving, or pulled them forward from the riverbanks with strong ropes.

Robert Fulton

Many round-trip journeys from the Upper Mississippi down to New Orleans and back took nine months. There had to be a better way to travel north against the current.

In 1807, a man named Robert Fulton built a new kind of wooden boat. Fulton's boat, called the *Clermont*, was powered by an engine fueled by steam hot enough to turn paddles on the side or back of the boat.

Some people called his boat "Fulton's Folly." (A *folly* is a crazy idea.) Others thought it would change river travel forever. They were right.

In 1811, a steamboat traveled along the Mississippi for the first time. Called the *New Orleans*, Fulton's newest boat began its journey in Pittsburgh, Pennsylvania. It traveled down the Ohio River and entered the Mississippi near Cairo, Illinois.

As it headed south to New Orleans, Fulton stopped from time to time and turned the boat around against the current. The boat moved upriver easily. No poles or ropes needed! From then on, a round-trip down and up the river would take about forty days instead of nine months.

Soon Fulton's new boat was shuttling back and forth between New Orleans and Natchez, Mississippi. Crowds gathered and hopped aboard at cities in between.

Shipbuilders in the East, especially in Pittsburgh, built more and more steamboats for passengers, as well as cargo. By the 1840s, boats overflowing with lumber, flour, corn, apples, and animals were making their way down the Ohio River to the bustling new Port of Saint Louis. Cotton, tobacco, whiskey, and other cargo was moved from the East along Southern rivers into the Mississippi and down to the Port of New Orleans.

Cargo was stored on the open lower deck. So were poorer passengers who were squeezed in between crates of vegetables, smelly livestock, and hot boilers. They brought their own food and slept on bales of cotton or sacks of grain.

Upstairs, the first-class accommodations were very different. On many boats, passengers who could afford the higher fare slept in fancy private rooms. Women dressed in expensive gowns. Men wore suits. They were served fine food and whiskey in beautiful dining rooms.

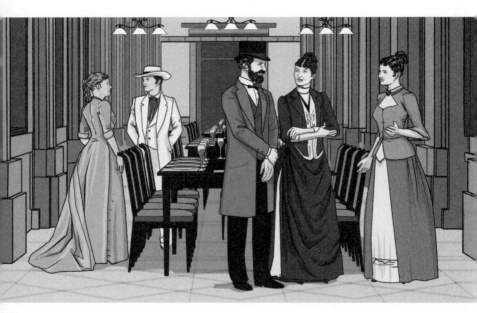

It didn't take long for word of these "floating palaces" to spread through cities along the Lower Mississippi. Everyone, it seemed, wanted to catch a ride to Memphis, Tennessee, where they could listen to street music that would later be called the blues. Others stayed aboard, gambling all the way to New Orleans.

Often, there were professional gamblers among the passengers. Many boarded in New Orleans and rode upriver, cheating money out of rich passengers. Furious victims complained, but river pilots had something important to attend to: the safety of their boats.

Pilots on the first steamboats had to learn how to avoid huge floating logs and branches, piles of sand—called *sandbars*—that had been formed by the currents, broken tree limbs, and pumpkins, timber, and everything else that had fallen off floating rafts. At first, collisions with other boats were common.

There were dangers aboard the boats as well. Open furnaces could spew cinders onto cotton bales and barrels, setting the wooden decks on fire. If the steam in boilers was too hot, it caused explosions, sending boat parts and passengers into the air.

Riding the River to Freedom

Because the Mississippi crossed slave states as well as free states, a steamboat could offer the means of escape. How did this happen? Slave owners would often rent out their slaves to work as extra crew on riverboats. Once aboard ships, the slaves saw from the other crew members (many were free black men) what a free life was like, so when a riverboat landed in a free state port, they jumped ship and fled. While some runaway slaves got help from members of the Underground Railroad once they reached the North, many were forced to find their own way to freedom.

Steamboat races were common, and also risky. Which boat would get to the next city first? Gamblers on the ships and along the riverbanks placed bets. Passengers begged the pilots to add more fuel and speed up. Push it harder, move it faster until sometimes, instead of winning, the pressure of the steam in the boiler caused a giant explosion.

By 1900, oil and coal had replaced wood fuel for the most part. There were fewer fires and explosions. Safety laws were passed. Steamboat races were no longer allowed. There were new laws about overcrowding and gambling. Many were pleased with the changes and the fact that boats became ever more luxurious. But others pined for the good old days, when riding the river had been dangerous and exciting.

The *Natchez* and the *Robert E. Lee*

One of the most famous steamboat races took place in 1870. Starting in New Orleans, the *Natchez* and the *Robert E. Lee* raced north to Saint Louis. Passing each other, they rushed around bends and tried to avoid rocks and logs without slowing down. At one point they collided, but kept on going.

One passenger said later: "I suddenly found myself standing face-to-face with a passenger on the other boat, and somewhat apparently to his surprise, extended my hand, and wished him a good morning."

The *Robert E. Lee* won, making the trip in three days. It was six hours ahead of the *Natchez*.

By the 1930s, the steamboat era was coming to an end. Railroads tracks snaked all over the United States now. It was easier to move freight by train. Before long, only tourists rode steamboats on the mighty Mississippi. They still do to this day.

CHAPTER 5
The Man Known as Mark Twain

"When I was a boy, there was but one permanent ambition among my comrades in our village on the west bank of the Mississippi River. That was, to be a steamboatman."
—Mark Twain, *Life on the Mississippi*

Like many river towns in the mid-1800s, Hannibal, Missouri, was a quiet, sleepy place. Some people called it boring. But young Samuel Langhorne Clemens wasn't like most people. He spent every free moment searching for adventure and excitement. To him, there was a world of magic not far from his family's house. It was called the Mississippi River.

Sam wasn't crazy about school. In fact, he often played hooky. But he loved to read. The books he liked best told stories of faraway places. When he wasn't reading, he headed down to the river.

Sam and his friends swam, built rafts, caught fish—walleye,

catfish, trout, sturgeon, and paddlefish—and explored caves.

As for Sam, nothing fascinated him as much as watching boats—keelboats and broadhorn barges came and went from the wharf. *Where are they heading?* he wondered. He had heard stories about exciting downriver cities like Saint Louis, Memphis, and New Orleans, and cities farther north, like Saint Paul, Minnesota, and Davenport, Iowa. What were these cities like? Were they like the places he had read about in books?

Keelboat

Steamboats were the most exciting boats. At night, Sam stayed awake, listening for the sound of their foghorns. During the day, he watched them go by, carrying goods and people, gray smoke billowing from their smokestacks, whistles blowing.

"Steamboat a-comin'," someone would call, and the quiet town would come alive. Doors flew open. Streets filled with people as they hurried down toward the wharf. Kids appeared from all directions and raced to the river.

On the wharf, Sam and his friends waited for

the deckhands to tie up the steamboat. Cargo and mail was unloaded. Passengers strolled off. Many had traveled to the Mississippi from other rivers, like the Illinois, Ohio, or the Missouri. For some, Hannibal was the last stop. Others were heading south to places Sam dreamed of visiting.

Music on the Mississippi

Besides books, the Mighty Miss has inspired countless songs—everything from sad ballads like "Ol' Man River," written for the Broadway musical *Show Boat* in 1927, to catchy tunes like "Mississippi Mud."

Country singer Johnny Cash lived about twenty miles west of the Mississippi. As a boy, he watched the water spill over the banks and spread out across the land. One of his most famous songs, "Five Feet High and Rising," tells the story of a river rising higher and higher.

From its birthplace in New Orleans, jazz spread to other cities, in part, thanks to the Mississippi River. How did this happen? In 1919, a seventeen-year-old black musician from New Orleans took a job playing cornet in a band on a riverboat traveling as far as Minneapolis. The musician's name was Louis Armstrong. A few years later he moved to Chicago, where some of his most famous records were produced.

Sam enjoyed talking to the passengers, but it was cabin boys, deckhands, cub pilots, engineers, and captains that he was waiting for. There was so much to learn. What kind of fuel was used to heat the steam in the boilers? What was beyond that bend downriver? How long did it take to get to New Orleans?

As for the pilot, he was the most interesting of all to Sam Clemens. Pilots were adventurous. They were loners who didn't talk much, yet people admired them.

Sam Clemens was determined to be a Mississippi River pilot someday.

Sam's early childhood was happy. His father was a judge. There was plenty of money. But then, when he was in the fifth grade, everything changed. Sam's father died. The money was gone. Sam would have to quit school and get a job.

Sam worked for a printer. He learned about letters and words and newspapers. Soon he was

writing funny little stories that were published in the local paper.

Sam never went back to school, but he kept on reading. Maybe, someday, he would be a writer when he wasn't being a river pilot.

In 1852, when Sam was seventeen years old, he packed his bags and headed south to Saint Louis where in time he found himself a job on a steamboat. As a cub pilot, he spent hours and hours watching the pilot, asking endless questions, struggling to understand each answer.

"My boy, you've got to know the shape of the river perfectly. It is all there is left to steer by on a very dark night. Everything else

is blotted out and gone. But mind you, it hasn't the same shape in the night that it has in the daytime.'

'How on earth am I ever going to learn it, then?'

'How do you follow a hall at home in the dark? Because you know the shape of it.'"

—Mark Twain, *Life on the Mississippi*

On April 9, 1859, Sam Clemens's dream came true. He became a fully licensed steamboat pilot. For two years he traveled the Mississippi, exploring all those faraway cities he had wondered about since he was a boy.

Sam loved being a pilot, but his time on the river didn't last long. In 1861, the Civil War began. The United States was at war with itself. Battles broke out along the Mississippi River. The river was closed to all traffic except military boats.

Mark Twain Chooses His Name

Sam Clemens became one of America's funniest and best-loved writers. He didn't write in a fancy way. He wrote plainly; his characters spoke the way real, everyday Americans did. Two of his most famous books are *The Adventures of Tom Sawyer* and *The Adventures of Huckleberry Finn*. In *Life on the Mississippi*, he told what it was like to grow up beside the river and learn to be a river pilot. In his books, he didn't use his real name. All of his books were published under the name Mark Twain. Many writers use names for their books that are different than their real names. They are called *pen names*. Sam Clemens chose a name from something he had learned on the river. River pilots lowered poles or lines into the water to measure how deep it was. Sometimes they'd call out, "Mark twain." Mark twain, or mark number two, was the second mark on the line or pole. It meant the water was twelve feet deep and safe enough to pass.

CHAPTER 6
The River at War

In 1860, Abraham Lincoln was elected the sixteenth president of the United States. The question that horribly divided the country was over slavery. Owning slaves was legal in Southern states, but in Northern states, it was against the law.

Abraham Lincoln

Lincoln was from the North. He hated slavery. He wanted to make slavery illegal in every state of the Union. Southern states believed that it was up to each state—not the president—to decide its own laws.

By 1861, eleven Southern states had decided to leave the United States and start their own government. They called it the Confederate States of America.

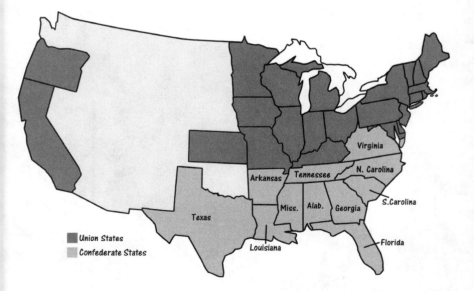

Union States
Confederate States

Virginia
Arkansas
Tennessee
N. Carolina
Miss. Alab. Georgia
S.Carolina
Texas
Louisiana
Florida

By April, America was at war. Northern Union soldiers were battling Southern Confederate soldiers. Both sides needed to bring supplies from Eastern states through the Gulf of Mexico to places farther west. Access to the Port of New Orleans was vital. (Louisiana was part of the Confederacy.)

In April 1862, the Union navy sailed in through the Gulf and made a surprise attack on the city. Confederate soldiers had expected them to arrive from the opposite direction—from the north. They had moved most of their troops out of New Orleans.

The Union won the battle easily.

Union soldiers and sailors were relentless. In the northern Mississippi River, the army and navy worked together. They moved along the river on paddle steamboats and marched in from the east. Battle by battle, they took over the river. Troops from the north captured New Madrid, Missouri, and Memphis, Tennessee. From New Orleans, they moved upriver to Baton Rouge, Louisiana, and to cities in Mississippi.

General Ulysses S. Grant was in charge of the Union troops in the area. There was one place he was determined to capture. If his troops could take Vicksburg, Mississippi, they would control the entire river. In the spring of 1863, Grant surprised the Confederates at Vicksburg. The battle raged for forty-seven days. When it was over, the Mississippi River belonged to the Union. It was one of the turning points in the Civil War.

Ulysses S. Grant

The war continued for two more years. Finally, on April 9, 1865, General Robert E. Lee, the leader of the Confederate troops, surrendered to General Ulysses S. Grant at the Appomattox Court House in Virginia. The Confederate states

were no longer a separate country. As before the
war, they were part of the United States.

Before long, the call of "Steamboat a-comin'"
could be heard along the river. Billowing smoke
drifted in the distance. The river was alive once
again.

CHAPTER 7
Locks, Tugs, and Waterfalls

Today, the Mississippi is one of the busiest rivers in the world. Lines of flat-bottomed barges carry containers of grain, coal, sand, gravel, corn, soybeans, wheat, and other cargo up and down the river. Some haul timber or concrete. Tugboats push the barges as they guide them from behind. Ferries take passengers from one side to the other. Log rafts float down the river. Cruise ships steam from town to town.

Piloting the Mississippi is not an easy job. The river widens and narrows and widens again and again. It is shallow in the headlands and deep in the South. In the upper river, pilots must make their way around rapids and waterfalls. Farther south, traffic increases as boats arrive from other rivers.

Flat-bottomed barges

The United States Army Corps of Engineers is in charge of the Mississippi. It is the job of these army soldiers to make sure boats can move safely and efficiently up and down the river. When there are problems, they think of ways to solve them. The engineers measure the height of bridges and the depth of the water so that river pilots will know

if it's too shallow for their boats to pass through. They design and build concrete dams that make places in the river deeper and wider. A *dam* is a wall across a river that can raise the water, hold it back, or move it in another direction. Twenty-nine concrete dams have been built to help river pilots move along the Upper Mississippi.

Waterfalls and rapids were a bigger problem to solve. How could pilots *navigate*—make their way—around them? Engineers decided to build locks that would help move boats higher or lower.

A *lock* is like an elevator in the river, but instead of cables moving an elevator car, water moves a boat up or down. Boats needing to move higher line up in the river and wait their turn. Sometimes large tugs and their barges have to wait for days. Boats wanting to enter the lock must first signal the lock operator and wait for a return signal to continue.

A flashing red light and long blast means DO NOT ENTER!

A flashing green light means ENTER.

The lock consists of two pools of water—one at the top and one at the bottom.

When a pilot gets the signal to go, gates open and the boat enters a space, like a chamber. Water from the upper pool flows into the lower pool through valves. As more water pours in the lower pool, the boat rises. When it reaches the upper pool, gates at the other end of the chamber open and the boat carries on.

Boats wanting to go down enter the upper pool. Water drains out, instead of in, through valves, until the upper pool is the same height as the lower pool and the boat can move on.

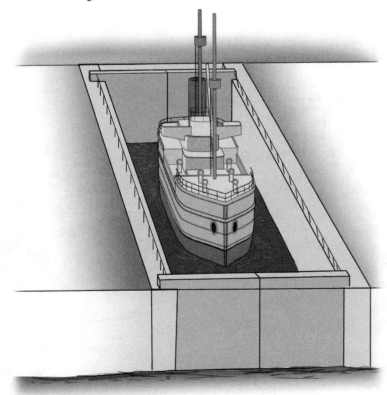

In the Lower Mississippi, between Baton Rouge, Louisiana, and the Gulf of Mexico, the water is deep enough for very big ships. Dams and locks are not necessary in this part of the river, but there are other problems for the engineers to solve. Large ships from all over the world enter

Southern ports. Huge steel ships called *tankers* carry large amounts of oil, gas, and other liquids to and from the Gulf of Mexico. The engineers keep the traffic moving smoothly. Tugboats help many of them maneuver to and from the dock. Trucks wait for the boats to unload and carry the cargo along highways all over the United States.

How a Tugboat Works

Tugboats, also called tugs, are the workhorses of the Mississippi River. They help other vessels maneuver through the water by pushing or pulling them. In the Lower Mississippi, tugs guide oil tankers and other large ships in and out of crowded harbors. Tugs push or tow log rafts and other boats through narrow canals. Some help break up ice so boats can move along the upper river in the winter.

CHAPTER 8
Disaster

Living beside a river can be interesting, exciting, and fun. But sometimes, when the rains come and the river pours onto the land, it can cause disasters. The Great Flood of 1927 was one of the worst floods ever recorded.

The rains began in the winter of 1926. Streams and rivers from the Rocky Mountains to the Appalachian Mountains swelled higher and wider. Water overflowed their banks and rolled downward. The rain kept falling, in the North, the West, the East, through the winter and into the spring, harder and harder.

People in Kansas, Oklahoma, Illinois, Kentucky, and other parts of the Mississippi River basin were worried. Would it ever let up?

It seemed like water was rushing downstream toward them from everywhere.

People who lived close to the Mississippi River were even more frightened. Swollen tributaries were draining so much water into the Mississippi. If the rain didn't stop, the Mighty Miss would overflow, too.

The rain kept falling. By March of 1927, the water in the Lower Mississippi was as high as the riverbanks. People were afraid the levees built by government workers would break. (*Levees* are walls along riverbanks built to hold back rising water.) What would happen if they collapsed? Water would flood the land.

Levees

The Army Corps of Engineers promised the levees would hold. Most people believed them. The engineers had built the levees, so they should know.

By April, the Lower Mississippi was at record highs and the water was still rising. People were told to leave their homes and head for higher ground. Many did. Others stayed. Later, as the water spilled from the river, the people who had stayed realized they had made a mistake. This flood was turning out to be worse than any other flood in history.

Then, on April 15, the rain began to fall all over Central and Southern states like Missouri, Illinois, Arkansas, Mississippi, Texas, and Louisiana. More than fourteen inches fell on New Orleans that day.

On April 16, 1927, the swollen Ohio brought even more water into the Mississippi at Cairo, Illinois. Thirty miles south, a twelve hundred–foot levee collapsed. Water from the river flooded 175,000 acres of land. Soon many more levees began to break. One after another, levees along the Mississippi River fell.

Churning, swelling water was exploding against levees on both sides of the Mississippi. People in towns on opposite sides of the river each hoped the other town's levee would collapse first. That side of the river would flood, but their side would be safe. There were fears of people sneaking across and knocking down a levee. Night after night, villagers stood guard.

In New Orleans, workers tried to keep back the water by blasting a hole in a levee. The plan worked. The water flowed through the hole to a safer place.

The town of Greenville, Mississippi, got the worst of it. The rain would not stop. Swift water from the Ohio, Missouri, and Arkansas Rivers had thundered into the swelling Mississippi. The water was coming. Greenville was in the worst possible spot it could be.

On April 21, river water near Greenville rose so high, it toppled all the levees, and by the next day the town was flooded with eight feet of water. Ten days after that, one million acres of nearby land were flooded ten feet high.

Some people left town to search for higher ground. Some climbed trees or waited for help on rooftops. Some scrambled to hold back the river by stacking sandbags to work as makeshift levees. But it was no use. The rain kept coming and the water continued to hurry across the land.

By the time the storm ended, twenty-seven thousand square miles of land in the middle of the United States was flooded.

One woman who was there wrote this account in a Greenville paper:

"As the water drew nearer it ceased to glitter, it was horrid, dirty water filled with bugs and crayfish and snakes and eels. The thought of that messy water coming into one's home was just too much to endure, and yet, there was not a thing on earth anyone could do except watch it come, to the street, to the walk, to the house, then up, up, steadily and inexorably up for a week."

It took a long time for the Mississippi River basin area to recover from the Great Flood of 1927. Some towns never were the same. Homes were washed away. Crops on either side of the Mississippi were destroyed. Big cities were under water.

Three hundred thirty thousand people had to be rescued from attics, treetops, and other high places. No one knows how many people died, but some people estimate it was as high as one thousand.

Something had to be done. More floods would come in the future. Some might even be worse than the Great Flood of 1927. It was clear that levees were not capable of holding back the river during huge storms.

A year later, the United States government passed the Flood Control Act of 1928. The Army Corps of Engineers would be in charge of finding new ways to control Mississippi River flooding. They did build stronger and higher levees in some places, but the engineers thought of other ways to control water and direct it away from cities. They remembered the hole that had been blasted in the New Orleans levee. Water had moved to a safer place. They decided to use the same idea to create spillways and floodways. *Spillways* are concrete structures by the river with many steel gates that can be opened to let out water safely. When the gates are open, water flows through floodway channels that have been

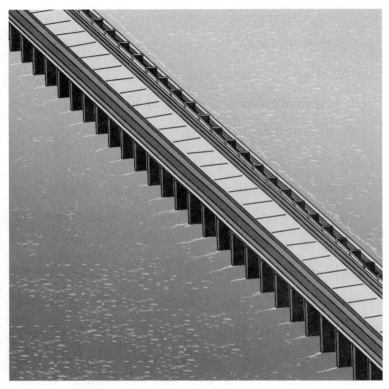

A spillway

cut in the land. *Floodway* paths lead to specially chosen safe areas of land.

Engineers would rather not flood any land, so Mississippi River spillways are only used in cases of extreme emergency.

The Morganza Spillway is about fifty miles north of Baton Rouge, Louisiana. It was completed in 1954, but it wasn't used until a massive flood in 1973. Forty-two of the 125 gates were opened to release the water and direct it away from the city. It worked.

New Orleans is a huge city that spreads out north of the Gulf of Mexico. It is difficult to protect New Orleans from flooding because water completely surrounds it. The Mississippi River flows right through it. There are canals throughout the city, and Lake Pontchartrain lies to its north. Also, the city is built on land shaped like a soup bowl; the deepest part of the "bowl" is below sea level. Levees had been built around the canals and the lake. But they were very old and needed repairs.

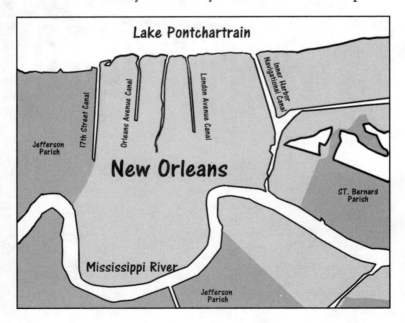

In 1931, the Army Corps of Engineers built the Bonnet Carré Spillway, thirty-three miles north of New Orleans. To this day, the spillway and floodways divert water away from the city center. Water travels through Lake Pontchartrain, and on to the Gulf of Mexico.

But sometimes, nothing can hold back the water.

On August 29, 2005, Hurricane Katrina, the third-strongest hurricane ever to hit the United States, raged across the Gulf Coast. Winds blew at more than one hundred miles per hour. Many places in Florida, Alabama, Mississippi, and Louisiana were devastated.

In New Orleans, the Mississippi River levees held. They didn't break. Some water did spill over the tops. That, however, was not the big problem. What caused so much damage and death was the collapse of levees around canals and the lake. Most of New Orleans ended up underwater. Nearly two thousand people died. Many left the city never to

return. Even now, there is still much rebuilding to do. New Orleans's location at the mouth of the Mississippi is why it became such a thriving, exciting city that tourists around the world flock to. However, its location has also been the reason for its near ruin.

CHAPTER 9
Keeping It Clean

The mighty Mississippi is one of the most magnificent rivers in the world.

Sixty percent of the birds in North America follow its path as they migrate north and south. Starlings, crows, doves, sandpipers, warblers, robins, mallards, Canada geese, and many other birds fly above it.

Bald eagles nest in white pine trees. River otters slide in and out of the water. Muskrats rest in lodges they have built in the river. Over two hundred species of fish swim in the river.

Fish and wildlife have depended on the Mississippi River for thousands of years. Native Americans fished there. They drank the water. Farms were small. Goods moved up and down the river on flatboats that used poles, not fuel.

When explorers and early settlers came to the river, its water was still clean enough to drink. But as more and more settlers came, problems arose for the river. Efforts to protect people hurt the Mississippi and surrounding areas. For example, some levees and dams blocked the river from reaching wetlands. The delta wetlands began to shrink. Habitats of plants, animals, and other wildlife began to disappear.

Cities throughout the Mississippi River basin grew larger and larger. Factories were built. They dumped waste and chemicals into the water. To

grow better crops, farmlands were sprayed with pesticides that make their way into the river water.

Tankers in the Lower Mississippi carried oil in and out of the river. Sometimes the oil spilled. Soon, the river water had to be cleansed, and distilled, to make it safe to drink. Fish and other wildlife died.

Every summer, a dead zone of about six thousand square miles forms from the mouth of the river into the Gulf of Mexico. Chemicals used to grow crops are washed into the Mississippi River and then flow down into the Gulf.

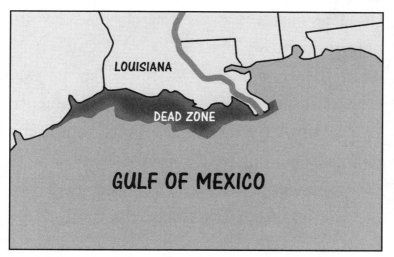

The fresh river water spreads across the saltwater and creates a condition that prevents oxygen in the water from reaching the lower layers of the Gulf. Every living thing needs oxygen to breathe. Dead seaweed clogs the bottom of the Gulf. Hardy fish can swim to the upper layers, but bottom-dwellers, like shrimp and worms, cannot survive.

More and more, people began to worry about what was happening to their river. They decided to do something. Locally, many formed groups that fight off pollution. They worked together to remove trash from the riverbanks. They urged Congress members in their states to pass laws to protect the Mississippi.

At the national level, a special agency was established in 1970. It is the Environmental Protection Agency. The EPA works to end pollution and other environmental problems all over the country. The Clean Water Act was passed in 1972. As the river changes, the Clean Water

Act changes, too. New laws are passed. Businesses and factories that pollute the river must pay fines. Farmers who use chemicals that pollute the river are fined, too.

The US Fish and Wildlife Service sets aside parts of the river called National Wildlife Refuges, to protect fish, plants, and wildlife. There are plans to rebuild protective wetlands and revitalize the Mississippi River delta with the creation of marshes and restoration of barrier islands and oyster reefs.

Someday, perhaps, the water in the mighty Mississippi will once again be as clean as it was when the early explorers noticed the great waters for the first time.

Timeline of the Mississippi River

19,000 BC	Ice sheets cover the area of the northern United States
10,000 BC	Last ice age ends, world warms up
AD 1541	Hernando de Soto and his men are the first Europeans to see the Mississippi River
1673	Father Jacques Marquette and Louis Joliet explore the river as far as present-day Arkansas
1682	René-Robert Cavelier, Sieur de La Salle journeys all the way down the river to the Gulf of Mexico
1803	France sells the Louisiana Territory to the United States
1807	Robert Fulton invents the steamboat
1811	The steamboat *New Orleans* travels from Pittsburgh to New Orleans
1859	Samuel Clemens—the real name of author Mark Twain—becomes a fully licensed steamboat pilot
1863	Union troops win the Battle of Vicksburg during the Civil War and gain control of the Mississippi River
1927	Greenville, Mississippi, is underwater due to the Great Flood of 1927
1928	US government passes the Flood Control Act of 1928
1970	Environmental Protection Agency is established
2002	Martin Strel swims the length of the river
2005	Hurricane Katrina devastates New Orleans and the Mississippi Gulf Coast

Timeline of the World

15,000 BC	*Homo sapiens* migrate across the Bering Strait into the Americas
4500 BC	Earliest known urban civilization arises in Sumer, in present-day Iraq
AD 1534	Jacques Cartier sails up the Saint Lawrence River
1543	Nicolaus Copernicus publishes his theory that the Earth revolves around the sun
1642	English Civil War begins
1800	Napoleon becomes first consul of France
1836	Mexican army defeats Texan defenders and takes control of the Alamo
1869	Suez Canal opens in Egypt
1892	Diesel engine patented
1908	Model T automobile produced by Ford Motor Company
1912	Ocean liner *Titanic* sinks on its maiden voyage
1927	Charles A. Lindbergh flies first successful solo nonstop flight from New York to Paris
1969	American astronaut Neil Armstrong is the first man to walk on the moon
1974	Richard M. Nixon becomes the first US president to resign from office
2006	The International Astronomical Union reclassifies Pluto as a dwarf planet

Bibliography

*Books for young readers

Barry, John M. *Rising Tide: The Great Mississippi Flood of 1927 and How It Changed America*. New York: Simon & Schuster, 1997.

Big River Man. Directed by John Maringouin. Los Angeles: Earthworks Films Inc., 2010, DVD.

*Brown, Don. *Drowned City: Hurricane Katrina & New Orleans*. New York: Houghton Mifflin Harcourt, 2015.

Heinrichs, Ann. *La Salle: La Salle and the Mississippi River*. North Mankato, MN: Compass Point Books, 2002.

Johnson, Robin. *The Mississippi: America's Mighty River*. Ontario, Canada: Crabtree Publishing Company, 2010.

Petersen, William J. *Steamboating on the Upper Mississippi*. Mineola, NY: Dover Publications, 1996.

Sandlin, Lee. *Wicked River: The Mississippi When It Last Ran Wild*. New York: Pantheon Books, 2010.

Schneider, Paul. *Old Man River: The Mississippi River in North American History*. New York: Henry Holt and Company, 2013.

The Valley of the Giant: Mississippi River Story. National Archives and Records Administration, 2007, DVD.

Twain, Mark. *Life on the Mississippi*. Boston: James R. Osgood & Company, 1883.

*Twain, Mark. *The Adventures of Huckleberry Finn*. London: Chatto & Windus, 1884.

*Twain, Mark. *The Adventures of Tom Sawyer*. Hartford, CT: American Publishing Company, 1876.

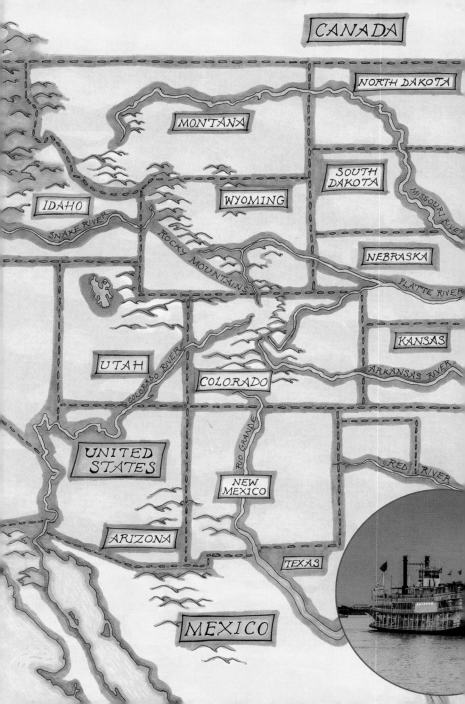

er in

The Mississippi River as it passes through Iowa

Paddlewheel riverboat on the Mississippi River

Mark Twain

A barge on the Mississippi Ri
Baton Rouge, Louisiana

MINNESOTA

WISCONSIN

ST. PAUL

MINNEAPOLIS

MISSISSIPPI RIVER

IOWA

MICHIGAN

OHIO

CHICAGO

ILLINOIS

INDIANA

OHIO RIVER

KENTUCKY

ST. LOUIS

MISSOURI

MISSISSIPPI RIVER

ARKANSAS

TENNESSEE

MEMPHIS

APPALACHIAN MOUNTAINS

NORTH CAROLINA

OKLAHOMA

SOUTH CAROLINA

ALABAMA

GEORGIA

MISSISSIPPI

LOUISIANA

NEW ORLEANS

FLORIDA